Poems That Build Character

Author	Karen Brown
Editor	Kathy Rogers
Artist	Mark Mason

About the Author

Karen Brown has been a teacher for 24 years. She has taught learning disabled and elementary students in Lee's Summit, Missouri. Karen has been a finalist in the Lee's Summit Teacher of the Year program and is listed in the *Who's Who of American Teachers*. She is a member of the International Reading Association, Parent-Teacher Association, and Society of Children's Book Writers and Illustrators.

Table of Contents

EP342 • ©2001 Edupress, Inc. • P.O. Box 883 • Dana Point, CA 92629
www.edupressinc.com
ISBN 1-56472-342-9
Printed in USA

Curriculum and Character Education

Across the nation, character education programs have become an integral part of the curriculum. Schools are actively developing programs to help students understand and develop commonly held ethical values and characteristics. Now you can link the development of good character to a standards-based, language arts curriculum.

The activities in *Poems That Build Character* will not only enhance students' reading and writing skills, they will develop their understanding and appreciation of the basic principles of good character. Increased awareness will be exhibited in the development of students' life skills in:

- Expressive and receptive communication skills, conflict resolution
- Coping with difficulties, recognizing boundaries, being flexible, maintaining perspective, being resilient, and deferring impulses
- Critical thinking, problem-solving, decision-making
- Anger management
- Courtesy, sharing, good manners, mutual respect, civility, and graciousness
- Insight, self-reflection, self-discipline, self-worth, self-respect, self-awareness, self-reliance, and self-management
- Relationship building within the family, in a work or school environment, between friends, and in the community
- Organization, leadership, time management, goal setting, work ethic, and accountability
- Appreciation of the differences among people
- Citizenship and civic responsibility
- Prevention of violence

About the Book

The poems were selected to represent the work of a variety of poets, classical and modern. Many titles and poets are included in Core Curriculum standards. Indexes are included to help match poems and activities to your state standards. Poem content reflects various moods, from serious to humorous.

Activities are designed to provide the opportunity for students to learn about various poetic forms. Use poems and activities as a springboard to learning about poetic forms, including:

Ballad—the oldest poetry form with regular rhyming patterns and meters; used for songs or the telling of stories

Blank verse—poetry form with non-rhyming lines all in regular meter

Free verse—poetry from that does not have to rhyme; stanzas may be different lengths, lines are usually different lengths, and there is no metrical pattern

Haikus and cinquains—poetry forms with a specific number of lines, each line containing a specific number of syllables

Every effort has been made to obtain permission to use previously published material. Any errors or omissions are unintentional.

How to Use the Book

Poems That Build Character is divided into two sections: ten lists of poems, each related to a particular character trait, and 20 activities that can be used in the study of any one or all of the character traits.

Each activity page is arranged for easy use in a literacy center. Teacher information and instructions are placed at the top of the page. Student instructions appear in a box on the lower half of the page. To use in a literacy center, cut off the teacher portion of the page and reproduce the student section. The student section may be laminated for extended use.

Traits of Good Character

For the purpose of this book, we have selected ten characteristics that are generally accepted as traits of good character: perseverance, respect, courage, trustworthiness, citizenship, fairness, responsibility, caring, honesty, and loyalty. The definition of each of these character traits is listed below, along with related traits that may be found in the teaching of character education.

Perseverance—Perseverance is the willingness to make a continuing, patient effort at getting something accomplished. Related traits are persistence and working hard.

Respect—Respect is a regard for the worth of someone or something. Respect includes respect for oneself, for the rights and dignity of other people, for laws and authority, and for the environment. Related traits are appreciation, understanding, and esteem.

Courage—Courage is the state of being fearless, unafraid, and brave. A person with courage is willing to face and deal with danger, trouble, or pain. Related traits are bravery and fortitude.

Trustworthiness—Trustworthiness is being deserving of trust. A trustworthy person is honest and can be depended upon. Related traits are promise-keeping and reliability.

Citizenship—Citizenship is the conduct or behavior of a person in relation to the group in which he lives. A good citizen is respectful of the rights, duties, and privileges of all citizens. Related traits are cooperativeness, fairness, and neighborliness.

Fairness—Fairness is the ability to makes decisions and judgments that are honest and impartial. A person who is fair is not influenced by self-interest, prejudice, or favoritism. Related traits are good sportsmanship and open-mindedness.

Responsibility—Responsibility is being accountable for actions and circumstances that are within a person's control. A responsible person takes care of himself and others, and fulfills his obligations. Related traits are self-discipline, dependability, and reliability.

Caring—Caring is an expression of love or regard. A person who is caring shows concern for other people. Related traits are compassion, understanding, empathy, consideration, and sympathy.

Honesty—Honesty means being truthful and upright. An honest person does not lie, cheat, or steal. Related traits are truthfulness and integrity.

Loyalty—Loyalty is the quality of being faithful to one's country, family, friends, duties, or beliefs. A loyal person follows through on his promises and commitments. Related traits are friendship and fidelity.

Decision Tree

Activity

Make a personal "Decision Tree."

Objective

The student will see how certain decisions lead to others through natural consequences.

Materials

• "Decision Tree" worksheet, next page
• Pen or pencil

Preparation

Students should be familiar with the "The Road Not Taken" by Robert Frost. (See page 36)

Thinking Levels

• Application
• Analysis
• Synthesis

Evaluation

The student will be able to think of a variety of choices and determine what consequences might result from each choice.

Student Instructions (for use in Literacy Centers)

Decision Tree

A "Decision Tree" will help you see how important it is to be careful in the choices you make.
One choice leads to another, and often you have to leave the unchosen paths behind.

Directions

1. Identify an important event that has occurred or might occur in your life. Write that event on the trunk of your "Decision Tree."

2. Think of a variety of solutions or decisions that you might make regarding this event. Write these solutions on the main branches of the tree.

3. On the smaller branches that off-shoot from the main branches, write consequences that might occur if you choose that solution. Add more small branches as necessary.

Example: Your event is *Education*. The branches might be *College, Technical School, No College*. The consequences of *No College* might be *Low-Paying Job, Unhappy at Work*.

4. Compare your tree with your classmates' and discuss the results.

Decision Tree

A Poem of Your Own

Activity

Write and illustrate a poem that represents a particular characteristic.

Objective

The student will be able to write a poem that applies to a character trait.

Materials

- Writing paper
- Pen or pencil
- Drawing paper
- Crayons or colored pencils

Preparation

Students should have studied some of the poems listed in the book and be familiar with poetry forms.

Thinking Levels

- Comprehension
- Application

Evaluation

Read the new poems to determine if the student understands that particular character trait's meaning.

Student Instructions (for use in Literacy Centers)

A Poem of Your Own

Write a poem that expresses the importance of one of the traits of good character!

Directions

1. Read some poems that relate to a character trait that you have selected.
2. Write an original poem that tells the importance of that character trait.
3. Illustrate your poem and present it to the rest of the class.

Analyze This

Activity

Analyze the structure of three or more poems by their beat and by rhyming or non-rhyming patterns.

Materials

- Copies of poems
- Highlighters
- Pen or pencil
- Writing paper

Thinking Levels

- Analysis

Objective

The student will be able to sort poems based on their structure.

Preparation

The students should be familiar with different styles of poems, counting syllables, and rhyming words.

Evaluation

The student will be able to identify the style of at least one poem.

Student Instructions (for use in Literacy Centers)

Analyze This

Learn more about poetry by analyzing syllable count and rhyming patterns!

Directions

1. Select a poem to analyze. Highlight any rhyming words in the poem. Count the number of syllables in each line, writing the number at the end of each line.

2. Analyze at least two more poems in the same way.

3. On the writing paper, write a comparison of the rhyming patterns and the syllable count for the poems you analyzed. Decide which poems have similar patterns based on your findings.

4. Look for additional poems that match the patterns you have found.

Real or Imaginary?

Activity

Identify real and make-believe characters in poetry. Label poems as fantasy, reality, or realistic fiction.

Materials

- Character outline, following
- Research materials
- Writing paper
- Pen or pencil

Thinking Levels

- Comprehension
- Evaluation

Objective

The student will be able to identify reality and fantasy within poems.

Preparation

Conduct a class discussion about the concepts of reality versus fantasy. Discuss the concept of "realistic fiction."

Evaluation

The student will be able to classify poems as fantasy, reality, or realistic fiction.

Student Instructions (for use in Literacy Centers)

Real or Imaginary?

Who is this poem talking about? Is it a real person or an imaginary character? Decide for yourself, then find out more about how that person represented traits of good character.

Directions

1. Read a selection of poems, identifying each as being reality, fantasy, or realistic fiction (a fictional story about an event that actually happened or a person who really lived).

2. Group your poems based on how you categorized them.

3. Select one of the characters from a poem that you have chosen.
   - If the person is real, find out more about that person's life and write a short biography.
   - If the character is from a fantasy poem, create a life story for that character.

4. Use the Character Outline page to write your biography. On the sheet, identify some of the character traits that this person has.

Character Outline

Title of poem:

Name of character:

Is this character real or fictional?

If the character is real, write a short biography. If the character is fictional, create in imaginary life story for him or her.

Identify two character traits that apply to this character. Explain what the character says or does that shows he or she has these traits.

Haikus

Teacher Instructions

Activity

Write a list of adjectives and adverbs that define a character trait and develop a haiku to describe it.

Materials

- Construction paper
- Writing paper
- Pen or pencil
- Crayons or colored pencils
- Glue or glue stick

Thinking Levels

- Comprehension
- Knowledge

Objective

The student will write a haiku about a character trait, showing knowledge of what the trait means.

Preparation

The students should know about adjectives and adverbs. They should also be familiar with the haiku as a poetry form. (Examples on pages 31, 54, and 57)

Evaluation

The haiku will properly describe the character trait and contain the correct number of syllables on each line.

Student Instructions (for use in Literacy Centers)

Haikus

A haiku is a Japanese poem. It has three lines that do not rhyme. The first line has five syllables, the second line seven syllables, and the third line five. Write a haiku about a character trait.

Directions

1. Select a character trait and make a list of adjectives and adverbs that describe it. Next to each word write the number of syllables the word contains.

2. Use the words in the list to create a haiku.
   - Begin by naming the character trait.
   - Write a five-syllable line to describe the trait.
   - Write a seven-syllable line.
   - Write another five-syllable line.
   - End by naming the character trait again.

4. Copy the haiku onto writing paper. Mount the writing paper on construction paper and illustrate your haiku with crayons or colored pencils.

Write a Story Poem

Activity

Write a "story" poem about an event in the student's life.

Objective

The student will tell a story in the form of a poem.

Materials

• Copy of "Paul Revere's Ride" (See page 34)
• Writing paper
• Pen or pencil

Preparation

This would be an excellent writing activity after a shared experience such as a field trip or a play.

Thinking Levels

• Application

Evaluation

The student will be able to realate a story in poem form.

Student Instructions (for use in Literacy Centers)

Write a Story Poem

Write a poem to tell the world about an exciting event in your own life!

Directions

1. Read the poem "Paul Revere's Ride."
2. Use short phrases to write down the sequence of events in the poem.
3. Think of an important event in your own life. Write short phrases that describe the sequence of what happened. If you want to, use the phrases to write a story of the event.
4. Using the poetic form of "Paul Revere's Ride," use the phrases and written story to create a poem that tells the story of the event.
5. Read your story poem to the rest of the class.

Letter to the Poet

Activity

Write a letter to a poet asking him how he creates his poems.

Materials

- Drawing paper
- Writing paper
- Pen or pencil
- Markers or crayons

Thinking Levels

- Knowledge
- Application

Objective

The student will familiarize himself with the art of writing poetry.

Preparation

Locate the mail address for the publishers of several of the poets represented in this book.

Evaluation

The students will be able to describe what a poet does or needs when writing a poem.

Student Instructions (for use in Literacy Centers)

Letter to the Poet

Where does a poet get his ideas? How does he write his poems? Many poets would be happy to answer your questions—you just have to ask!

Directions

1. Before starting, brainstorm a list of questions you want to ask. For example:
   - How many hours a day do you write?
   - Where do you do your writing?
   - Do you use a computer when you write?

2. If a poet is still living, he or she can be reached by writing to their publisher. Select your poet, then find out how to contact him or her.

3. Write a letter to your poet, asking the questions on your list. Include a self-addressed stamped envelope with your letter to make it easy for your poet to respond.

Story-Writing

Teacher Instructions

Activity

Develop a story that incorporates one of the poems in the book.

Materials

- Writing paper
- Pen or pencil
- Drawing paper
- Markers or colored pencils

Thinking Levels

- Knowledge
- Synthesis

Objective

The student will show an understanding of a poem by using it as part of a short story.

Preparation

The students should have read many of the poems in this book.

Evaluation

The student will create a story that appropriately uses a poem as part of the story's plot or dialogue.

Student Instructions (for use in Literacy Centers)

Story-Writing

Sometimes the meaning of a poem is more clear if the poem is presented within a story!

Directions

1. Select a poem that suggests a story idea to you. Decide what kind of person would be speaking in the poem. What circumstances might be taking place?
2. Write a short story that illustrates what is happening when the poem is spoken. Perhaps you could use the poem as dialogue.
3. Illustrate your story and display the poem and short story together.
4. Read your short story aloud to the rest of the class.

Poet Biography

Activity

Select a poet and research his or her life. Write a short biography, describing the character traits that you think makes the poet successful.

Materials

- Library or internet access
- Other research materials
- Pen or pencil
- Writing paper

Thinking Levels

- Comprehension
- Analysis
- Evaluation

Objective

The student will relate how a poet has used specific character traits.

Preparation

Students should familiarize themselves with the lives of several of the poets in the book in order to make a decision about which person they would like to study in more detail.

Evaluation

The student will be able to analyze and defend the characteristics that they feel the person exhibits in his or her life.

Student Instructions (for use in Literacy Centers)

Poet Biography

Choose a poet who writes poems that you like. Do some research about the poet's life.
Write a biography that tells about the positive character traits that describe that poet's life.

Directions

1. Select a poet. Use reference materials or the internet to get information about the poet's life. Think about what character traits made the poet's life successful.

2. Write a biography that tells about the poet's life and describes the character traits you selected. Explain how the character traits were expressed in the poet's life.

3. Copy one of the poems by your selected poet onto writing paper. Display the poem and the biography together.

Character Categories

Teacher Instructions

Activity

Sort a variety of poems by their character traits into the correct category.

Materials

- Poems
- Character trait headings
- Pen or pencil
- Paper

Thinking Levels

- Comprehension
- Knowledge
- Analysis

Objective

The student will be able to categorize the traits and poems.

Preparation

Duplicate one or more pages of poems from different character trait sections. Cut apart the individual poems. Use poster board to make tent-like cards naming the individual character traits.

Evaluation

The student will later be given the same cut-apart sheets, and will sort at least 80% of them correctly.

Student Instructions (for use in Literacy Centers)

Character Categories

Can you determine which character trait each poem is talking about?
Test your knowledge by sorting poems into the correct category.

Directions

1. Work with a partner or in a small group. Sort the poems from the headings. Lay the headings out in a row on the table.

2. Together, read each poem and place it in a row underneath the heading for the character trait you believe the poem describes.

3. When all of the poems have been sorted, write a list of the character traits with the titles of the individual poems that go with each trait.

4. Compare your list with the original, uncut pages, or have a class discussion where everyone shares and compares their lists.

Capitalize and Punctuate

Teacher Instructions

Activity

Study how punctuation marks and capital letters are used in poetry.

Materials

• Copies of poems
• Yellow, red, blue, green, orange, and pink highlighters or markers
• Worksheet, following

Thinking Levels

• Knowledge
• Analysis

Objective

The student will notice a difference in capitalization and punctuation rules for poems as opposed to stories.

Preparation

Duplicate one or more pages of poems for students to write on.

Evaluation

The student will recognize patterns and differences in punctuation and capitalization in poetry versus other types of writing.

Student Instructions (for use in Literacy Centers)

Capitalize and Punctuate

Poems and stories—are the punctuation rules the same?

Directions

1. Select a page of poems and read the poems carefully.
2. Use markers or highlighters to do the following:
   • Circle all capital letters in yellow
   • Circle all periods in red
   • Circle all commas in blue
   • Circle all question marks in green
   • Circle all exclamation points in orange
   • Circle all quotation marks in pink
3. Rewrite at least two of the poems in paragraph form, using correct punctuation. Highlight the punctuation marks as in Step #2.
3. Use the worksheet to analyze how capitalization and punctuation rules change when writing poetry and paragraphs.

G A ? Capitalize and Punctuate ! J D

M Study the poems you read and the paragraphs you wrote. Write a rule about using: R

• Capital letters in poems _____

U _____ P

_____

• Capital letters in paragraphs _____

_____

_____

• Commas in poems _____

_____

_____

• Commas in paragraphs _____

_____

_____

• Periods in poems _____

_____

_____

• Periods in paragraphs _____

_____

_____

On the back of this page, write rules about how another punctuation mark is used differently in poetry than it is in paragraph writing. Examples: *quotation mark, question mark, exclamation point.*

Act It Out

Teacher Instructions

Activity

Write a skit or short play based on one of the poems and act it out.

Materials

• Poems
• Writing paper
• Pen or pencil
• Student-supplied props

Thinking Levels

• Synthesis

Objective

The student will be able to create and act out situations or poems involving specific character traits.

Preparation

Provide copies of the poems in this book. Plan for writing and preparation time. Establish a time for presentation of the skits.

Evaluation

The students can be evaluated by the way in which the skit portrays the value or the poem.

Student Instructions (for use in Literacy Centers)

Act It Out

Create a skit or a short play based on one of the poems or based on a specific character trait.

Directions

1. In a small group, select a poem or a character trait that you would like to portray.
2. Write a skit that either portrays the story of the poem or that demonstrates the character trait it represents.
3. Make a list of props and/or costumes that the students in your group will need. Make arrangements to bring them to class.
4. Practice, then present your skit to the rest of the class.

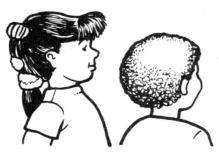

Rhyming Words

Activity

The students will make lists of rhyming words to be used in an original poem.

Materials

• Rhyming word dictionary
• Writing paper
• Pen or pencil
• Copies of poems
• Highlighter

Thinking Levels

• Application

Objective

The student will become familiar with the use of rhyming words when writing poetry.

Preparation

Review rhyming words with students. Discuss the use of beat, syllables, and alliteration.

Evaluation

The student will able to use rhyming words and patterns of poetry to write an original poem.

Student Instructions (for use in Literacy Centers)

Rhyming Words

Lots of poems contain rhyming words. Create your own list of words that rhyme, then write a poem using them!

Directions

1. Read some poems from the book, using a highlighter to mark words that rhyme with each other. Also notice the beat, syllables, and alliteration of each line.

2. Make lists of one-, two-, three-, and four-syllable words relating to a specific character trait.

3. Read your poem aloud to a partner to help in "hearing" the beat of the lines. Edit your poem to make it sound its best.

4. Read your poem aloud to the rest of the class.

A Poem a Day

Activity

Read and explain a poem that relates to the character trait being studied.

Materials

- Copies of poems
- Writing paper
- Pen or pencil

Thinking Levels

- Application
- Analysis

Objective

The student will relate how a character trait is portrayed within the poems. They will compare and contrast how the character traits are used in a variety of poems.

Preparation

It is best to select the poems you would most like the students to read. You may want to make up a weekly schedule for the order of character traits that you would like to study.

Evaluation

Student should be able to show how the values are used in various poems and be able to share the poem's meaning with the class.

Student Instructions (for use in Literacy Centers)

A Poem a Day

Discussing a poem with other students will make it easier to understand.
Prepare an oral presentation that will help other students understand the poem you read.

Directions

1. Form a group of two to four students. Within your group, assign a reader, writer, notetaker, and speaker (each student may need to take more than one role).

2. The reader reads the selected poem to the group. As you discuss the meaning of the poem within the group, the notetaker writes down notes of what is said. When the discussion is over, the writer will neatly write the group's conclusions about the poem.

3. The reader then reads the poem to the entire class. The speaker uses the notes written to explain the discussion that took place and presents the conclusions reached by the small group.

School Song

Activity

Write a school song, pledge, or poem emphasizing the traits of good character.

Objective

The student will create their own poem, pledge, or song emphasizing character traits.

Materials

• Writing paper
• Pen or pencil
• Rhyming dictionary

Preparation

The students will need to be familiar with how to write a poem and know the present school song and/or pledge. They should have read many poems included in this book.

Thinking Levels

• Comprehension
• Application
• Analysis

Evaluation

The student should be able to create a short poem or verse implementing some of the traits of good character.

Student Instructions (for use in Literacy Centers)

School Song

A school song or pledge tells everyone what character traits the students are trying to live up to. Write a song or pledge that represents your school's ideals.

Directions

1. Form a small group and work together to decide whether to create a song or a pledge.

2. As a group, write the song or pledge and decide on how you will present it to the class (for example, a live performance, a poster, a banner).

Journal Activity

Activity

Write a journal page about how a specific character trait was used. Find a poem or stanza of a poem that expresses that character trait.

Materials

• Journal page, following
• Pen or pencil

Thinking Levels

• Application
• Synthesis
• Evaluation

Objective

The student will be able to reflect daily about how values are used in their lives.

Preparation

Duplicate the journal page for student use. Set aside time for journal activity if it is not already part of the classroom schedule.

Evaluation

Read the journal weekly to determine whether the student understands the concepts taught and can apply them in daily life instances.

Student Instructions (for use in Literacy Centers)

Journal Activity

Use a journal to record events that you think show the use of good character traits.

Directions

1. Be on the lookout each day for times when you use values that have been studied, or when you observe other people using those values.

2. Use a journal page to record your observations. Select a poem or a stanza of a poem that relates to the value you observe and write it on your journal page. Store your journal page in a folder.

3. After a few days, read your journal entries. As part of your journal activity, write a poem that talks about your observations.

Journal Page

_____

_____

_____

_____

_____

_____

_____

_____

_____

_____

_____

_____

_____

_____

_____

_____

_____

_____

_____

Caring

Caring is an
expression of love
or regard.

The Gulf
Katherine Mansfield

A Gulf of silence separates us from each other.
I stand at one side of the gulf, you at the other.
I cannot see you or hear you, yet know that
   you are there.
Often I call you by your childish name
And pretend that the echo to my crying is your
   voice.
How can we bridge the gulf? Never by speech
   or touch.
Once I thought we might fill it quite up with
   tears.
Now I want to shatter it with our laughter.

Let Me Give
Anonymous

I do not know how long I'll live
But while I live, Lord, let me give
Some comfort to someone in need
By smile or nod, kind word or deed.

And let me do what ever I can
To ease things for my fellow man.
I want naught but to do my part
To "lift" a tired or weary heart.

To change folks' frowns to smiles again.
Then I will not have lived in vain
And I'll not care how long I'll live
If I can give...and give...and give.

The Canary
Elizabeth Turner

Mary had a little bird,
With feathers bright and yellow,
Slender legs—upon my word,
He was a pretty fellow!

Sweetest notes he always sung,
Which much delighted Mary;
Often where his cage was hung,
She sat to hear Canary.

Crumbs of bread and dainty seeds
She carried to him daily,
Seeking for the early weeds,
She decked his palace gaily.

This, my little readers, learn,
And ever practice duly;
Songs and smiles of love return
To friends who love you truly.

A Time To Talk
Robert Frost

When a friend calls to me from the road
And slows his horse to a meaning walk,
I don't stand still and look around
On all the hills I haven't hoed,
And shout from where I am, What is it?
No, not as there is a time to talk.
I thrust my hoe in the mellow ground,
Blade-end up and five feet tall,
And plod: I go up to the stone wall
For a friendly visit.

How Do I Love Thee?
Elizabeth Barrett Browning

How do I love thee? Let me count the ways.
  I love thee to the depth and breadth and height
My soul can reach, when feeling out of sight
  For the ends of Being and ideal Grace.
I love thee to the level of every day's
  Most quiet need, by the sun and candlelight.
I love thee freely, as men strive for Right;
  I love thee purely, as they turn from Praise.
I love with a passion put to use
  In my old griefs, and with my childhood's faith.
I love thee with a love I seemed to lose
  With my lost saints,—I love thee with the breath,
Smiles, tears, of all my life!—and, if God choose,
  I shall but love thee better after death.

Remember
Christina Rossetti

Remember me when I am gone away,
  Gone far away into the silent land;
When you can no more hold me by the hand,
  Nor I half turn to go, yet turning stay.
Remember when no more, day by day,
  You tell me of our future that you planned:
Only remember me; you understand
  It will be late to counsel then and pray.

Yet if you should forget me for a while
  And afterwards remember, do not grieve;
For if the darkness and corruption leave
  A vestige of the thoughts that once I had,
Better by far you should forget and smile
  Than that you should remember and be sad.

Grow Old Along with Me
Robert Browning

Grow old along with me!
The best is yet to be,
The last of life, for which the first was
  made:
Our times are in His hand
Who saith "A whole I planned,
Youth shows but half; trust God: see all, nor
  be afraid!"

Life's Scars
Ella Wheeler Wilcox

They say the world is round, and yet
  I often think it's square,
So many little hurts we get
  From corners here and there.
But one great truth in life I've found,
  While journeying to the West—
The only folks who really wound
  Are those we love the best.

The man can thoroughly despise
  Can rouse your wrath, 'tis true;
Annoyance in your heart will rise
  At things mere strangers do;
But those are only passing ills;
  This rule all lives will prove;
The ranking wound which aches and thrills
  Is dealt by hands we love.

The choicest garb, the sweetest grace,
  Are oft to strangers shown;
The careless mien, the frowning face,
  Are given to our own.
We flatter those we scarcely know,
  We please the fleeting guest,
And deal full many a thoughtless blow
  To those who love us best.

Love does not grow on every tree,
  Nor true hearts yearly bloom.
Alas for those who only see
  This cut across the tomb!
But, soon or late, the fact grows plain
  To all through sorrow's test;
The only folks who give us pain
  Are those we love the best.

Solitude
Ella Wheeler Wilcox

Laugh, and the world laughs with you;
  Weep, and you weep alone.
For the sad old earth must borrow its mirth,
  But has trouble enough of its own.
Sing, and the hills will answer;
  Sigh, it is lost on the air.
The echoes bound to a joyful sound,
  But shrink from voicing care.

Rejoice, and men will seek you;
  Grieve, and they will turn and go.
They want full measure of all your pleasure,
  But they do not need your woe.
Be glad, and your friends are many;
  Be sad, and you lose them all.
There are none to decline your nectared wine,
  But alone you must drink life's gall.

Feast, and your halls are crowded;
  Fast, and the world goes by.
Succeed and give, and it helps you live,
  But no man can help you die.
There is room in the halls of pleasure
  For a long and lordly train,
But one by one we must all file on
  Through the narrow aisle of pain.

If I Can Stop One Heart from Breaking
Emily Dickinson

If I can stop one heart from breaking,
I shall not live in vain;
If I can ease one life the aching,
Or cool one pain,
Or help one fainting robin
Unto his nest again,
I shall not live in vain.

The Day is Done
Henry Wadsworth Longfellow

The day is done, and the darkness
  Falls from the wings of night
As a feather wafted downward
  From the eagle in his flight.

I see the light of the village
  Gleam through the rain and the mist,
And the feeling of sadness comes o'er me
  That my soul cannot resist:

Come, read to me some poem,
  Some simple and heartfelt lay,
That shall soothe the restless feeling,
  And banish the thoughts of the day.

Not from the grand old masters,
  Not from the bards sublime,
Whose distant footsteps echo
  Through the corridors of time.

For, like the strains of martial music,
  Their mighty thoughts suggest
Life's endless toil and endeavor;
  And tonight I long for rest.

Read from the humbler poet,
  Whose songs gushed from his heart,
As showers from the clouds of summer,
  Or tears from the eyelids start;

Who, through long days of labor,
  And nights devoid of ease,
Still heard his soul the music
  Of wonderful melodies.

Such songs have power to quiet
  The restless pulse of care,
And come like the benediction
  That follows after prayer.

Then read the treasured volume
  The poem of my choice,
And lend to the rhyme of the poet
  The beauty of thy voice.

And the night shall be filled with music,
  And the cares, that infest the day,
Shall fold their tents, like the Arabs,
  And as silently steal away.

The Return
Emily Dickinson

Though I get home how late, how late!
So I get home, 't will compensate.
Better will be the ecstasy
That they have done expecting me,
When, night descending, dumb and dark,
They hear my unexpected knock.
Transporting must the moment be,
Brewed from decades of agony!
To think just how the fires will burn,
Just how long-cheated eyes will turn
To wonder what myself will say,
And what itself will say to me,
Beguiles the centuries of way!!

My Mother
Ann Taylor

Who fed me from her gentle breast,
And hushed me in her arms to rest,
And on my cheek sweet kisses prest?
    My Mother.

When sleep forsook my open eye,
Who was it sung sweet hushaby,
And rocked me that I should not cry?
    My Mother.

Who sat and watched my infant head,
When sleeping in my cradle bed,
And tears of sweet affection shed?
    My Mother.

When pain and sickness made me cry,
Who gazed upon my heavy eye,
And wept, for fear that I should die?
    My Mother.

Who dressed my doll in clothes so gay,
And fondly taught me how to play,
And minded all I had to say?
    My Mother.

Who ran to help me when I fell,
And would some pretty story tell,
Or kiss the place to make it well?
    My Mother.

Who taught my infant lips to pray,
And love God's holy book and day,
And walk in wisdom's pleasant way?

    My Mother.

And I ever cease to be
Affectionate and kind to thee,
Who was so very kind to me,
    My Mother?

Ah no! the thought I cannot bear,
And if God please my life to spare,
I hope I shall reward thy care,
    My Mother.

When thou art feeble, old, and grey,
My healthy arm shall be thy stay,
And I will soothe thy pains away,
    My Mother.

And when I see thee hang thy head,
'Twill be my turn to watch thy bed,
And tears of sweet affection shed,
    My Mother.

For could our Father in the skies
Look down with pleased or loving eyes,
If ever I could dare despise
    My Mother?

Trustworthiness

Being trustworthy means being deserving of trust.

Our Heroes
Phoebe Cary

Here's a hand to the boy who has courage
　To do what he knows to be right;
When he falls in the way of temptation,
　He has a hard battle to fight.
Who strives against self and his comrades
　Will find the most powerful foe.
All honor to him if he conquers.
　A cheer for the boy who says "NO!"

There's many a battle fought daily
　The world knows nothing about;
There's many a brave little soldier
　Whose strength puts a legion to rout.
And he who fights sin singlehanded
　Is more of a hero, I say,
Than he who leads soldiers to battle
　And conquers by arms in the fray.

Be steadfast, my boy, when you're tempted,
　To do what you know to be right.
Stand firm by the colors of manhood,
　And you will o'ercome in the fight.
"The right," be your battle cry ever
　In waging the warfare of life,
And God, who knows who are the heroes,
　Will give you the strength for the strife.

Trustworthiness
Anonymous

Waves upon the shore.
Splashing with a constant beat
Through the steps of time.

Trusting Butterfly
Claire Boiko

Hold your breath—
Don't come too near!
She's just about to land
　Ah!
A butterfly has honored me
By resting on my hand.
Birds fly from us great humans.
And beetles scuttle past,
Antennas quivering just as if
Each moment were their last.
How wise, how kind, she makes me feel!
For, pausing on her jaunt
From flower to tree,
She's choosing me
To be her confidant!

I Have a Bird in Spring
Emily Dickinson

I have a Bird in Spring
　Which for myself doth sing—
And as the summer nears—
　And as the Rose appears,
Robin is gone.

Yet do I not repine
　Knowing that Bird of mine
Though flown—
　Learneth beyond the sea
Melody new for me
　And will return.

Fast is a safer hand
　Held in a truer Land
Are mine—
　And though they now depart,
Tell I my doubting heart
　They're thine.

In a serener Bright,
　In a more golden light
I see
　Each little doubt and fear,
Each little discord here
　Removed.

Then will I not repine,
　Knowing that Bird of mine
Though flown
　Shall in a distant tree
Bright melody for me
　Return.

The Boy We Want
Anonymous

A boy that is truthful and honest
And faithful and willing to work;
But we have not a place that we care to
　disgrace
With a boy that is ready to shirk.

Wanted—a boy you can tie to,
A boy that is trusty and true,
A boy that is good to old people,
And kind to the little ones too.

A boy that is nice to the home folks,
And pleasant to sister and brother,
A boy who will try when things go awry
To be helpful to father and mother.

These are the boys we depend on—
Our hope for the future, and then
Grave problems of state and the world's
　work await
Such boys when they grow to be men.

The Reminder
Thomas Hardy

While I watch the Christmas blaze
　Paint the room with ruddy rays,
Something makes my vision glide
　To the frosty scene outside.

There, to reach the rotting berry,
　Toils a thrush,—constrained to very
Dregs of food by sharp distress,
　Taking such with thankfulness.

Why, O starving bird, when I
　One day's joy would justify,
And put misery out of view,
　Do you make me notice you!

If

Rudyard Kipling

If you keep your head when all about you
   Are losing theirs and blaming it on you;
If you can trust yourself when all men doubt you,
   But make allowance for their doubting too;
If you can wait and not be tired by waiting,
   Or, being lied about, don't deal in lies,
Or, being hated, don't give way to hating,
   And yet don't look too good, nor talk too wise;

If you can dream—and not make dreams your master;
   If you can think—and not make thoughts your aim;
If you meet with triumph and disaster
   And treat those two imposters just the same;
If you can bear to hear the truth you've spoken
   Twisted by knaves to make a trap for fools,
Or watch the things you gave your life to broken,
   And stoop and build' em up with wornout tools;

If you can make one heap of all your winnings
   And risk it on one turn of pinch-and-toss,
And lose, and start again at your beginnings
   And never breathe a word about your loss;
If you can force your heart and nerve and sinew
   To serve your turn long after they are gone,
And so hold on when there is nothing in you
   Except the Will which says to them: "Hold on!";

If you can talk with crowds and keep your virtue,
   Or walk with kings—nor lose the common touch;
If neither foes nor loving friends can hurt you;
   If all men count with you, but none too much;
If you can fill the unforgiving minute
   With sixty seconds' worth of distance run—
Yours is the earth and everything that's in it,
   And—which is more—you'll be a man my son!

Courage

The Charge of the Light Brigade
Alfred, Lord Tennyson

Half a league, half a league,
Half a league onward
All in the valley of Death
Rode the six hundred.
'Forward, the Light Brigade!
Charge for the guns!' he said:
Into the valley of Death
Rode the six hundred

'Forward, The Light Brigade!'
Was there a man Dismay'd?
Not tho' the soldier knew
  Some one blunder'd:
Their's not to make reply,
Their's but to do and die:
Into the valley of Death
  Rode the six hundred.

Cannon to right of them,
Cannon to left of them,
Cannon in front of them
  Volley'd and thunder'd;
Storm'd at the shot and shell,
Boldly they rode and well,
Into the jaws of Death,
Into the mouth of Hell
  Rode the six hundred.

Flash'd all their sabres bare,
Flash'd as they turn'd in air
Sabring the gunners there,
Charging an army, while
  All the world wonder'd

Courage is the state of being fearless, unafraid, and brave.

Plunged in the battery-smoke
Right thro' the line they broke;
Cossack and Russian
Reel'd from the sabre-stroke
  Shatter'd and sunder'd
Then they rode back, but not
  Not the six hundred

Cannon to right of them,
Cannon to left of them,
Cannon behind them
  Volley'd and thunder'd
Storm'd at with shot and shell,
While horse and hero fell,
They that had fought so well
Came thro' the jaws of Death,
Back from the mouth of Hell,
All that was left of them,
  Left of six hundred.

When can their glory fade?
O the wild charge they made!
  All the world wonder'd.
Honour the charge they made!
Honour the Light Brigade,
  Noble six hundred!

A Psalm of Life
Henry Wadsworth Longfellow

Tell me not, in mournful numbers,
  Life is but an empty dream!
For the soul is dead that slumbers
  And things are not what they seem.
Life is real! Life is earnest!
  And the grave is not its goal;
Dust thou art, to dust returnest,
  Was not spoken of the soul.
Not enjoyment, and not sorrow,
  Is our destined end or way;
But to act, that each to-morrow
  Find us farther than to-day.
Art is long, and Time is fleeting,
  And our hearts, though stout and brave,
Still, like muffled drums are beating
  Funeral marches to the grave.
In the world's broad field of battle,
  In the bivouac of Life,
Be not like dumb, driven cattle!
  Be a hero in the strife!
Trust no Future, howe'er pleasant!
  Let the dead Past bury its dead!
Act,—act in the living Present!
  Heart within, and God o'erhead!
Lives of great men all remind us
  We can make our lives sublime,
And, departing, leave behind us
  Footprints on the sands of time;
Footprints, that perhaps another
  Sailing o'er life's solemn main,
A forlorn and shipwrecked brother,
  Seeing, shall take heart again.
Let us, then, be up for any fate;
  Still achieving, still pursuing,
Learn to labor and to wait.

The Road Not Taken
Robert Frost

Two roads diverged in a yellow wood,
  And sorry I couldn't travel both
And be one traveler, long I stood
  And looked down one as far as I could
To where it bent in the undergrowth;
  Then took the other, as just as fair,
And having perhaps the better claim,
  Because it was grassy and wanted wear;
Though as for that the passing there
  Had worn them really about the same,
And both that morning equally lay
  In leaves no step had trodden black.
Oh, I kept the first for another day!
  Yet knowing how way leads on to way,
I doubted if I should ever come back.
  I shall be telling this with a sigh
Somewhere ages and ages hence:
  Two roads diverged in a wood, and I—
I took the one less traveled by,
  And that has made all the difference.

Do You Fear the Wind?
Hamlin Garland

Do you fear the force of the wind,
  The slash of the rain?
Go face them and fight them,
  Be savage again.
Go hungry and cold like the wolf.
  Go wade like the crane.
The palms of your hands will thicken.
  The skin of your cheek will tan.
You'll grow ragged and weary and swarthy.
  But you'll walk like a man!

Paul Revere's Ride
Henry Wadsworth Longfellow

Listen my children and you shall hear
  Of the midnight ride of Paul Revere,
On the eighteenth of April, in Seventy-five;
  Hardly a man is now alive
Who remembers that famous day and year.
  He said to his friend, "If the British march
By land or sea from the town to-night,
  Hang a lantern aloft in the belfry arch
Of the North Church tower as a signal light,
  One if by land, and two if by sea;
And I on the opposite shore will be,
  Ready to ride and spread the alarm
Through every Middlesex village and farm,
  For the country folk to be up and to arm."
Then he said "Good-night!" and with muffled oar
  Silently rowed to the Charlestown shore,
Just as the moon rose over the bay,
  Where swinging wide her moorings lay
The Somerset, British man-of-war;
  A phantom ship, with each mast and spar
Across the moon like a prison bar,
  And a huge black hulk, that was magnified
By its own reflection in the tide.
  Meanwhile, his friend through alley and street
Wanders and watches, with eager ears,
  Till in the silence around him he hears
The muster of men at the barrack door,
  The sound of arms, and the tramp of feet,
And the measured tread of the grenadiers,
  Marching down to their boats on the shore.
Then he climbed the tower of the Old North Church,
  By the wooden stairs, with stealthy tread,
To the belfry chamber overhead,
  And startled the pigeons from their perch
On the sombre rafters, that round him made
  Masses and moving shapes of shade,
By the trembling ladder, steep and tall
  To the highest window in the wall,

Where he paused to listen and look down
  A moment on the roofs of the town
And the moonlight flowing over all.
  Beneath, in the church yard, lay the dead,
In their night encampment on the hill,
  Wrapped in silence so deep and still
That he could hear, like a sentinel's tread,
  The watchful night-wind, as it went
Creeping along from tent to tent,
  And seeming to whisper, "All is well!"
A moment only he feels the spell
  Of the place and the hour, and the secret dread
Of the lonely belfry and the dead;
  For suddenly all his thoughts are bent
On a shadowy something far away,
  Where the river widens to meet the bay,
A line of black that bends and floats
  In the rising tide like a bridge of boats
Meanwhile, impatient to mount and ride,
  Booted and spurred, with a heavy stride
On the opposite shore walked Paul Revere.
  Now he patted his horse's side,
Now he gazed at the landscape far and near,
  Then, impetuous, stamped the earth,
And turned and titled his saddle girth;
  But mostly he watched with eager search
The belfry tower at the Old North Church,
  As it rose above the graves on the hill,
Lonely and spectral and somber and still.

And lo! as he looks, on the belfry's height
  A glimmer, and then a gleam of light!
He springs to his saddle, the bridle he turns,
  But lingers and gazes, till full on his sight
A second lamp on the belfry burns.

  A hurry of hoofs in a village street,
A shape in the moonlight, a bulk in the dark,
  And beneath, from the pebbles, in passing, a spark
Struck out by a steed flying fearless and fleet;
  That was all! And yet, through gloom and the light,
The fate of a nation was riding that night;
  And the spark struck out by the steed, in his flight,
Kindled the land into flame with its heat.

  He has left the village and mounted the steep,
And beneath him, tranquil and broad and deep,
  Is the Mystic, meeting the ocean tides;
And under the alders that skirt its edge,
  Now soft on the sand, now loud on the ledge,
Is heard the tramp of his steed as he rides.

  It is twelve by the village clock
When he crossed the bridge into Medford town.
  He heard the crowing of the cock,
And the barking of the farmer's dog,
  And felt the damp of the river fog,
That rises after the sun goes down.

  It was one by the village clock,
When he galloped into Lexington.
  He saw the gilded weathercock
Swim in the moonlight as he passed,
  And the meeting-house windows, black and bare,
Gaze at him with a spectral glare,
  As if they already stood aghast
At the bloody work they would look upon.
  It was two by the village clock,
When he came to the bridge in Concord town.
  He heard the bleating of the flock,
And the twitter of birds among the trees,
  And felt the breath of the morning breeze
Blowing over the meadow brown.
  And one was safe and asleep in his bed
Who at the bridge would be first to fall,

Who that day would be lying dead,
Pierced by a British musket ball.
  You know the rest. In the books you have read
How the British regulars fired and fled,
  How the farmers gave them ball for ball,
From behind each fence and farmyard wall,
  Chasing the redcoats down the lane,
Then crossing the fields to emerge again
  Under the trees and the turn of the road,
And only pausing to fire and load.
  So through the night rode Paul Revere;
And so through the night went his cry of alarm
  To every Middlesex village and farm,
A cry of defiance, and not of fear,
  A voice in the darkness, a knock at the door,
For, borne on the night-wind of the Past,
  Through all our history, to the last,
In the hour of darkness and peril and need,
  The people will waken and listen to hear
The hurrying hoof-beats of that steed,
  And the midnight message of Paul Revere.

Honesty

My Excuse
David L. Harrison
(reprinted with permission of the author)

But I did do my homework!
Yes ma'am!
I really really did!
Un-huh.
Mama wrapped fish bones in it.
See?
She really really did!
Un-huh.
And them old fish bones
Stinked up the kitchen
Till Daddy threw 'em out.
Un-huh!
Now our neighbor, she's old,
And she's got an old cat,
And she got in our trash can.
See?
So my brother run past me
And past the old man
And he grabbed them fish bones
From that old cat
And he run home grinnin'!
But we all held our noses
'Cause it smelled bad!
His hand, not my homework.
So Daddy he took
And buried it in the yard.
No ma'am.
My homework, not my brother's hand.
And I couldn't do nothin' about it.
So see?
And by then it was late.
Really really late!
There wasn't nothin' I could do!
And that's purely the truth!
Yes ma'am!
Un-huh!

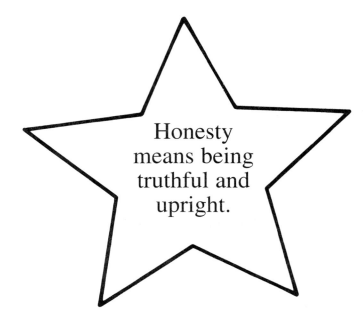

Honesty means being truthful and upright.

Truth Never Dies
Anonymous

Truth never dies. The ages come and go.
The mountains wear away, the stars retire.
Destruction lays earth's mighty cities low;
And empires, states and dynasties expire;
But caught and handed onward by the wise,
Truth never dies.

Though unreceived and scoffed at through the
  years;
Though made the butt of ridicule and jest;
Though held aloft for mockery and jeers,
Denied by those of transient power possessed,
Insulted by the insolence of lies,
Truth never dies.

It answers not. It does not take offense,
But with mighty silence bides its time;
As some great cliff that braves the elements
And lifts through all the storms its head
  sublime,
It ever stands, uplifted by the wise;
And never dies.

As rests the Sphinx amid Egyptian sands;
As looms on high the snowy peak and crest;
As firm and patient as Gibralter stands,
So truth, unwearied, waits the era blessed
When men shall turn to it with great surprise.
Truth never dies.

The Character of a Happy Life
Henry Wotton

How happy is born and taught,
  That serveth not another's will;
Whose armor is his honest thought,
  And simple truth his utmost skill!

Whose passions not his masters are,
  Whose soul is still prepared for death,
Untied unto the worldly care
  Of public frame, or private death;

Who envies none that chance doth raise,
  Or vice; who never understood
How deepest wounds are given by praise;
  Nor rules of state, but rules of good:

Who hath his life from rumors freed,
  Whose conscience is his strong retreat;
Whose state can neither flatterers feed,
  Nor ruins make oppressors great;

Who God doth late and early pray,
  More of his grace and gifts to lend;
And entertains the harmless day
  With a religious book or friend

This man is freed from servile bands,
  Of hope to rise, or fear to fall;
Lord of himself, though not of lands;
  And having nothing, yet hath all.

Truth
Ben Jonson

Truth is the trial of itself,
And needs no other touch;
And purer than the purest gold,
Refine it ne'er so much.

It is the life and light of love,
The sun that ever shineth,
And spirit of that special grace,
That faith and love defineth.

It is the warrant of the word,
That yields a scent so sweet,
As gives a power to faith to tread
All falsehood under feet.

Truth the Best
Elizabeth Turner

Yesterday Rebecca Mason,
  In the parlour by herself,
Broke a handsome china basin,
  Placed upon the mantelshelf.
Quite alarmed, she thought of going
  Very quietly away,
Not a single person knowing
  Of her being there that day.
But Rebecca recollected
  She was taught deceit to shun;
And the moment she reflected,
  Told her mother what was done;
Who commended her behavior,
  Loved her better, and forgave her.

Respect

Respect is a regard for the worth of someone or something.

O Captain! My Captain!
Walt Whitman

O Captain! My Captain! Our fearful trip is
   done.
The ship has weather'd every rack, the prize
   we sought is won,
The port is near, the bells I hear, the people
   all exulting,
While follow eyes the steady keel, the
   vessel grim and daring;
But O heart! heart! heart!
O the bleeding drops of red,
Where on the deck my Captain lies,
Fallen cold and dead.

O Captain! my Captain! Rise up and hear
   the bells;
Rise up—for you the flag is flung—for you
   the bugle trills,
For you bouquets and ribbon'd wreaths—
   for you the shores a-crowding,
For you they call, the swaying mass, their
   eager faces turning;
Here Captain! dear father!
This arm beneath your head!
It is some dream that on the deck,
You've fallen cold and dead.

My captain does not answer, his lips are
   pale and still,
My father does not feel my arm, he has no
   pulse nor will,
The ship is anchor'd safe and sound, its
   voyage closed and done,
From fearful trip to victor ship comes in
   with object won;
Exult O shores, and ring O bells!
But I with mournful tread,
Walk the deck my Captain lies,
Fallen cold and dead.

What Man May Learn, What Man May Do
Anonymous

What man may learn, what man may do,
   Of right or wrong of false or true,
While, skipper-like, his course he steers
   Through nine and twenty mingled years,
Half misconceived and half forgot,
   So much I know and practice not.

Old are the words of wisdom, old
   The counsels of the wise and bold:
To close the ears, to check the tongue,
   To keep the pining spirit young;
To act the right, to say the true,
   And to be kind whate'er you do.

Thus we across the modern stage
   Follow the wise of every age;
And, as oaks grow and rivers run
   Unchanged in the unchanging sun,
So the eternal march of man
   Goes forth on an eternal plan.

You are Old, Father William
Lewis Carroll

"You are old, father William," the young man said,
"And your hair has become very white;
And yet you incessantly stand on your head—
Do you think, at your age, it is right?"

"In my youth," father William replied to his son,
"I feared it would injure the brain;
But now that I'm perfectly sure I have none,
Why, I do it again and again."

"You are old," said the youth, "as I mentioned before,
And have grown most uncommonly fat;
Yet you turn a back-somersault in at the door—
Pray, what is the reason of that?"

"In my youth," said the sage, as he shook his grey locks,
"I kept all my limbs very supple
By the use of this ointment—one shilling the box—
Allow me to sell you a couple."

"You are old," said the youth, "and your jaws are too weak
For anything tougher than suet;
Yet you finish the goose, with the bones and the beak—
Pray, how did you manage to do it?"

"In my youth," said his father, "I took to the law,
And argued each case with my wife;
And the muscular strength, which it gave to my jaw,
Has lasted the rest of my life."

"You are old," said the youth; "one would hardly suppose
That your eye was as steady as ever;
Yet you balanced an eel on the end of your nose—
What made you so awfully clever?"

"I have answered three questions, and that is enough,"
Said the father; "don't give yourself airs!
Do you think I can listen all day to such stuff?
Be off, or I'll kick you down stairs!"

Somebody's Mother
Anonymous

The woman was old, and ragged, and gray,
  And bent with the chill of the winter's day;

The street was wet with the recent snow,
  And the woman's feet were aged and slow.

She stood at the crossing and waited long,
  Alone, uncared for, amid the throng

Of human beings who passed her by,
  Nor heeded the glance of her anxious eye.

Down the street, with laughter and shout,
  Glad in the freedom of "school let out,"

Came the boys like a flock of sheep,
  Hailing the snow piled white and deep.

Past the woman so old and gray
  Hastened the children on their way,

Nor offered a helping hand to her—
  So meek, so timid, afraid to stir

Lest the carriage wheels or the horses' feet
  Should crowd her down on the slippery street.

At last came one of the merry troop—
  The gayest laddie of all the group;

He paused beside her and whispered low,
  "I'll help you across if you wish to go."

Her aged hand on his strong arm
  She placed, and so, without hurt or harm,

He guided the trembling feet along,
  Proud that his own were firm and strong.

Then back again to his friends he went,
  His young heart happy and well content.

"She's somebody's mother, boys, you know,
  For all she's aged and poor and slow;

"And I hope some fellow will lend a hand,
  To help my mother, you understand,

"If ever she's poor and old and gray,
  When her own dear boy is far away."

And "somebody's mother" bowed low her head
  In her home that night and the prayer she said

Was, "God, be kind to the noble boy
  Who is somebody's son and pride and joy!"

Face to Face
Anita E. Posey

I'd like to go around the world
  And get a chance to see
The boys and girls of other lands
  And let them all see me.

I'd like to meet them face to face,
  And get to know their names.
I'd like to sit and talk with them
  And learn to play their games.

I'd like to visit in their homes,
  Their family life to share.
I'd like to taste the food they eat,
  And see the clothes they wear.

I'd like to get to know them well
  Before my journey's end;
For only when you know someone
  Can he become your friend.

And so, someday, I'd like to go
  Around the world and see
The boys and girls of other lands
  And let them all see me.

Kindness to Animals
Anonymous

Little children, never give
  Pain to things that feel and live;
Let the gentle robin come
  For the crumbs you save at home;
As his meat you throw along
  He'll repay you with a song.
Never hurt the timid hare
  Peeping from her green grass lair,
Let her come and sport and play
  On the lawn at close of day.
The little lark goes soaring high
  To the bright windows of the sky,
Singing as if 'twere always spring,
  And fluttering on an untired wing—
Oh! let him sing his happy song,
  Nor do these gentle creatures wrong.

Trees
Joyce Kilmer

I think that I shall never see
  A poem so lovely as a tree.

A tree whose hungry mouth is prest
  Against the earth's sweet flowing breast.

A tree that looks at God all day
  And lifts her leafy arms to pray.

A tree that may in summer wear
  A nest of robins in her hair;

Upon whose bosom snow has lain:
  Who intimately lives with rain.

Poems are made by fools like me,
  But only God can make a tree.

The Man in the Glass
Anonymous

When you get what you want in your
  struggle for self
And the world makes you king for a day,
Just go to a mirror and look at yourself,
And see what that man has to say.

For it isn't your father or mother or wife,
Who judgement upon you must pass;
The fellow whose verdict counts most in
  your life
Is the one staring back from the glass.

He's the fellow to please, never mind all
  the rest,
For he's with you clear up to the end,
And you've passed the most dangerous,
  difficult test
If the man in the glass is your friend.

You may fool the whole world down the
  pathway of years.
And get pats on the back as you pass,
But your final reward will be heartaches
  and tears
If you've cheated the man in the glass.

Woodman, Spare That Tree!
George Pope Morris

Woodman, spare that tree!
  Touch not a single bough!
In youth it sheltered me,
  And I'll protect it now.
'Twas my forefather's hand
  That placed it near his cot;
There, woodman, let it stand,
  Thy axe shall harm it not!

That old familiar tree,
  Whose glory and renown
Are spread o'er land and sea,
  And wouldst thou hew it down?
Woodman, forbear thy stroke!
  Cut not its earth-bound ties;
O, spare that aged oak,
  Now towering to the skies!

When but an idle boy
  I sought its grateful shade;
In all their gushing joy
  Here too my sisters played.
My mother kissed me here;
  My father pressed my hand—
Forgive this foolish tear,
  But let that old oak stand!

My heart-strings round thee cling,
  Close as thy bark, old friend!
Here shall the wild-bird sing,
  And still thy branches bend.
Old tree! the storm still brave!
  And, woodman, leave the spot;
While I've a hand to save,
  Thy axe shall hurt it not.

A Distant Drummer
Henry David Thoreau

If a man does not keep pace
with his companions
perhaps it is because he
hears
a different drummer.
Let him step to the music
he hears
however measured
or far away.

Fable
Ralph Waldo Emerson

The mountain and the squirrel
  Had a quarrel,
And the former called the latter "Little Prig,"
  Bun replied,
"You are doubtless very big;
  But all sorts of things and weather
Must be taken in together,
  To make up a year
And a sphere.
  And I think it no disgrace
To occupy my place.
  If I'm not so large as you,
You are not small as I,
  And not half so spry.
I'll not deny you make
  A very pretty squirrel track;
Talents differ; all is well and wisely put;
  If I cannot carry forests on my back,
Neither can you crack a nut.

Fairness

Fairness is
making
decisions that
are impartial.

"But That's Not Fair!"
Karen Brown

My little sister is such a pest.
  She follows me wherever I go.
Why mom won't make her stop right now
  I'll never, ever know.

"Don't follow me," I yell at her.
  I tell my mom, "You just don't care."
Mom says, "You know she worships you!"
  I say, "But that's not fair!"

No matter what I have or I get,
  With her, Mom always makes me share.
"Be generous to your sissy, Dear."
  I say, "But that's not fair!"

Whatever I decide to do
  My sister has to do it, too.
Why is she such a copy cat?
  I haven't got a clue.

I think my mom loves Sissy best.
  She always lets her make a mess.
I have to clean up all by myself
  And Mom seems to care less.

That pest is getting on my nerves.
  I always am the one to lose.
My mother thinks that I should try
  To walk in Sissy's shoes.

My older sister's mean to me,
  Although I love her very much.
She never lets me play with her,
  Hold hands and kiss and such.

I try to get my mom to make
  My older sister play with me.
"Sis needs to play with kids her age!"
  "But that's not fair, Mommy!"

Whenever we play school or house,
  I always have to be the baby,
I wish I'd be the older one.
  That sounds more fair to me.

My sister gets to go to school
  And has a teacher all her own.
She learns to read and spell and write.
  Not fair, how much she's grown.

I think my Mom loves Sissy best.
  There's lots of stuff in her baby book.
I hardly have a thing in mine.
  Don't trust me? Take a look.

I have to wear her hand-me-downs.
  I never get anything brand new.
I hate the clothes that she outgrows.
  I wish she never grew.

Our mother calls us in one day,
  "We're having baby number three."
"But that's not fair!" we shout and whine.
  For once we both agree.

Poems That Build Character   © EDUPRESS, INC   EP342

The Rainy Day
Henry Wadsworth Longfellow

The day is cold, and dark, and dreary;
  It rains, and the wind is never weary;
But at every gust the dead leaves fall,
  And the day is dark and dreary.

My life is cold, and dark, and dreary;
  It rains, and the wind is never weary;
My thoughts still cling to the moldering Past,
  But my hopes of youth fall thick in the blast,
And the day is dark and dreary.

Be still, sad heart! and cease repining;
  Behind the clouds is the sun still shining;
Thy fate is the common fate of all,
  Into each life some rain must fall,
Some days must be dark and dreary.

Thought
Walt Whitman

Of Equality—As if it harm'd me, giving
  others the same chances and
rights as myself—As if it were not
  indispensable to my own
rights that others possess the same.

The Runaway Slave
Walt Whitman

The runaway slave came to my house and stopt outside,
  I heard his motions crackling the twigs of the woodpile,
Through the swung half-door of the kitchen I saw him limpsy and weak,
  And went where he sat on a log and led him in and assured him,
And brought water and fill'd a tub for his sweated body and bruis'd feet,
  And gave him a room that enters from my own, and gave him some coarse clean clothes.
And remember perfectly well his revolving eyes and his awkwardness,
  And remember putting plasters on the galls of his neck and ankles;
He staid with me a week before he was recuperated and pass'd north.
  I had him sit next me at table, my fire-lock lean'd in the corner.

Grab-Bag

Helen Hunt Jackson

A fine game is Grab-bag, a fine game to see!
For Christmas, and New Year, and birthdays,
    and all.
Happy children, all laughing and screaming
    with glee!
If they draw nothing more than a pop-corn ball.
'T is a prize they welcome with eyes of
    delight,
And hold it aloft with a loud, ringing cheer;
Their arms waving high, all so graceful and
    white;
Their heads almost bumping, so close and so
    near.
The laughter grows louder; the eyes grow more
    bright.
Oh, sweet is the laughter, and gay is the
    sight—
A fine game is Grab-bag! a fine game to see!

A strange game of Grab-bag I saw yesterday;
I'll never forget it as long as I live.
Some street-beggars played it,—poor things,
    not in play!
A man with a sack on his back, and a sieve,—
A poker to stir in the barrels of dirt,—
A basket to hold bits of food he might find,—
'T was a pitiful sight, and a sight that hurt,
But a sight it is well to keep in one's mind.

His children were with him, two girls and
    three boys;
Their heads held down close, and their eyes all
    intent;
No sound from their lips of glad laughter's gay
    noise;
No choice of bright playthings to them the
    game meant!
A chance of a bit of waste cinder to burn;
A chance of a crust of stale bread they
    could eat;
A chance—in a thousand—as chances return—
Of ragged odd shoes they could wear on their
    feet!

The baby that yet could not totter alone,
And snatched at the morsels he thought looked
    the best.
The sister that held him, oppressed by his
    weight—
Herself but an over-yeared baby, poor child!—
Had the face of a woman, mature, sedate,
And looked but the older whenever she smiled.

Oh, a sad game is Grab-bag—a sad game to
    see!
As beggars must play it, and their chances fall;
When Hunger finds crusts an occasion for glee,
And Cold finds no rags too worthless or small.
O children, whose faces have shone with
    delight,
As you played at your Grab-bag with shouting
    and cheer,
And stretched out your arms, all so graceful
    and white,
And gayly bumped heads, crowding near and
    more near,
With laughter and laughter, and eyes growing
    bright,—
Remember this picture, this pitiful sight,
Of a sad game of Grab-bag—a sad game
    to see!

Loyalty

Barbara Frietchie
John Greenleaf Whittier

Up from the meadows rich with corn,
  Clear in the cool September morn,
The clustered spires of Frederick stand
  Green-walled by the hills of Maryland.
Round about them orchards sweep,
  Apple and peach tree fruited deep,
Fair as the garden of the Lord
  To the eyes of the famished rebel horde,
On the pleasant morn of early fall
  When Lee marched over the mountain wall;
Over the mountains winding down,
  Horse and foot, into Frederick town.
Forty flags with their silver stars
  Forty flag with their crimson bars
Flapped in the morning wind; the sun
  Of noon looked down, and saw not one.
Up rose old Barbara Frietchie then,
  Bowed with her fourscore years and ten;
Bravest of all in Frederick town,
  She took up the flag the men hauled down;
In her attic window the staff she set,
  To show that one heart was loyal yet.
Up the street came the rebel tread,
  Stonewall Jackson riding ahead.
Under his slouched hat left and right
  He glanced; the old flag met his sight.
"Halt!"—the dust-brown ranks stood fast.
  "Fire!"—out blazed the rifle blast.
It shivered the window, pane and sash;
  It rent the banner with seam and gash.
Quick, as it fell, from the broken staff

Loyalty is being faithful to
one's country, family,
friends, duties,
or beliefs.

Dame Barbara snatched the silken scarf.
She leaned far out the window-sill,
  And shook it forth with a royal will.
"Shoot, if you must, this old gray head,
  But spare your country's flag," she said.
A shade of sadness, a blush of shame,
  Over the face of the leader came;
The nobler nature within him stirred
  To life at the woman's deed and word;
"Who touches a hair of yon gray head
  Dies like a dog! March on!" he said.
All day long through Frederick street
  Sounded the tread of marching feet;
All day long that free flag tost
  Over the heads of the rebel host.
Ever its torn folds rose and fell
  On the loyal winds that loved it well;
And through the hill-gaps sunset light
  Shone over it with a warm good-night.
Barbara Freitchie's work is o'er,
  And the rebel rides on his raids no more.
Honor to her! And let a tear
  Fall, for her sake, on Stonewall's bier.
Over Barbara Freitchie's grave,
  Flag of freedom and Union, wave!
Peace and order and beauty draw
  Round thy symbol of light and law;
And ever the stars above look down
  On thy stars below in Frederick town!

Heroes We Never Name
M. Lucille Ford

Back on the men of honor
  Enrolled on the scroll of fame,
Are the millions who go unmentioned—
  The heroes we never name!
Those who have won us the victories,
  And conquered along the way;
Those who have made us a nation—
  A tribute to them I would pay.

Back to our nation's first leader,
  Of Lincoln and Wilson, too,
Back of the mind directing our course
  Was the army that carried it through.
Back of the generals and captains
  Was the tramping of rank and file,
And back of them were the ones at home
  Who labored with tear and with smile.

And what of the "everyday" heroes
  Whose courage and efforts ne'er cease!
Toilers who struggle and labor and strive
  And hope for a future of peace?
Hats off to the worthy leaders;
  Their honor I'd ever acclaim—
But here's a cheer for the many brave,
  The heroes we never name!

Day of Memories
Emma W. Little

This is a day of memories
Of loyal hearts, and true,
Of hearts that beat like ours today,
Of hearts that loved, of hearts that longed
To live and sing, to work and play.

Now have come years of peace again,
Of lasting peace we pray.
Still may we honor in our songs
That loyal band who for our land
Died, hoping still to write its wrongs.

The Thousandth Man
Rudyard Kipling

One man in a thousand, Solomon said,
Will stick more close than a brother.
And it's worth while seeking him half
  your days
If you find him before the other.
Nine hundred and ninety-nine depend
On what the world sees in you,
But the Thousandth man will stand your friend
With the whole round world agin you.

'Tis neither promise nor prayer nor show
Will settle the finding for 'ee.
Nine hundred and ninety-nine of 'em go
By your look, or your acts, or your glory,
But if he finds you and you find him,
The rest of the world don't matter;
For the Thousandth Man will sink or swim
With you in any water.

You can use his purse with no more talk
Than he uses yours for his spendings,
And laugh and meet your daily walk
As though there had been no lendings.
Nine hundred and ninety-nine of 'em all,
Because you can show him your feelings.

His wrong's your wrong, and his right's your
  right,
In season or out of season.
Stand up and back it in all men's sight—
With that for you only reason!
Nine hundred and ninety-nine can't bide
The shame or mocking or laughter,
But the Thousandth Man will stand by
  your side
To the gallows-foot—and after!

Little Boy Blue
Eugene Field

The little town dog is covered with dust,
But sturdy and staunch he stands;
And the little toy soldier is red with rust,
And his musket molds in his hands.
Time was when the little toy dog was new
And the soldier was passing fair;
And that was the time that our Little Boy Blue
Kissed them and put them there.

"Now, don't you go till I come," he said,
"And don't you make any noise!"
So, toddling off to his trundle-bed,
He dreamed of the pretty toys;
And as he was dreaming, an angel song
Awakened our Little Boy Blue—
Oh! the years are many, the years are long,
But the little toy friends are true!

Aye, faithful to Little Boy Blue they stand,
Each time in the same old place—
Awaiting the touch of a little hand,
And the smile of a little face;
And they wonder, as waiting these long years
  through
In the dust of that little chair,
What has become of our Little Boy Blue,
Since he kissed them and put them there.

In Flanders Fields
John McCrae

In Flanders fields the poppies blow
  Between the crosses, row on row,
That mark our place; and in the sky
  The larks, still bravely singing, fly
Scarce heard amid the guns below.
  We are the Dead. Short days ago
We lived, felt dawn, saw sunset glow,
  Loved and were loved, and now we lie
In Flanders Fields.

Take up our quarrel with the foe;
  To you from failing hands we throw
The torch; be yours to hold it high.
  If ye break faith with us who die
We shall not sleep, though poppies grow
  In Flanders Fields.

Friendship's Rule
M. Lucille Ford

Our teacher says there is a rule
We should remember while in school,

At home, at play, whate'er we do,
And that's the rule of friendship true.

If you would have friends, you must do
To them the kindly things that you

Would like to have them do and say
To you while you're at work or play.

And that's the rule of friendship true;
It works in all we say and do.

It pays to be a friend polite,
For friendship's rule is always right.

Citizenship

Citizenship is the conduct of a person in relation to the group in which he lives.

The House by the Side of the Road
Sam Walter Foss

There are hermit souls that live withdrawn
In the place of their self-content;
There are souls like stars, that dwell apart, in a
fellowship firmament;
There are pioneer souls that blaze their paths
Where highways never ran—
But let me live by the side of the road
And be a friend to man.

Let me live in a house by the side of the road

Where the race of men go by—
The men who are good and the men who
are bad,
As good and as bad as I,
I would not sit in the scorner's seat,
Or hurt the cynic's ban—
Let me live in a house by the side of the road
And be a friend to man.

I see from my house by the side of the road,

By the side of the highway of life,
The men who press with the ardor of hope,
The men who are faint with the strife.
But I turn not away from their smiles nor
their tears,
Both part of an infinite plan—
Let me live in a house by the side of the road
And be a friend to man.

I know there are brook-gladdened meadows ahead

And mountains of worrisome height;
That the road passes on through the long
afternoon
And stretches away to the night.
But still I rejoice when the travelers rejoice,
And weep with the strangers that moan,
Nor live in my house by the side of the road
Like a man who dwells alone.

Let me live in my house by the side of the road—

It's here the race of men go by.
They are good, they are bad, they are weak, they
are strong,
Wise, foolish—so am I;
Then why should I sit in the scorner's seat,
Or hurl the cynic's ban?
Let me live in my house by the side of the road
And be a friend to man.

Poems That Build Character   © EDUPRESS, INC   EP342

Mending Wall

Robert Frost

Something there is that doesn't love a wall,
That sends the frozen-ground-swell under it,
And spills the upper boulders in the sun;
And makes gaps even two can pass abreast.
The work of hunters is another thing:
I have come after them and made repair
Where they have left not one stone on a stone,
But they would have the rabbit out of hiding,
To please the yelping dogs. The gaps I mean,
No one has seen them made or heard them
　made,
But at spring mending-time we find them
　there.
I let my neighbour know beyond the hill;
And on a day we meet to walk the line
And set the wall between us once again.
We keep the wall between us as we go.
To each the boulders that have fallen to each.
And some are loaves and some so nearly balls
We have to use a spell to make them balance:

"Stay where you are until our backs are
　turned!"
We wear our fingers rough with handling them.
Oh, just another kind of out-door game,
One on a side. It comes to little more:
There where it is we do not need the wall:
He is all pine and I am apple orchard.
My apple trees will never get across
And eat the cones under his pines, I tell him.
He only says, "Good fences make good
　neighbors."
Spring is the mischief in me, and I wonder
If I could put a notion in his head:
"Why do they make good neighbours? Isn't it
Where there are cows? But here there are
　no cows.
Before I built a wall I'd ask to know
What I was walling in or walling out,
And to whom I was like to give offence.
Something there is that doesn't love a wall,
That wants it down." I could say "Elves"
　to him,
But it's not elves exactly, and I'd rather
He said it for himself. I see him there
Bringing a stone grasped firmly by the top
In each hand, like an old-stone savage armed.
He moves in darkness as it seems to me,
Not of woods only and the shade of tree.
He will not go behind his father's saying,
And he likes having thought of it so well
He says again, "Good fences make good
　neighbours."

I Hear America Singing
Walt Whitman

I HEAR America singing, the varied carols I hear;
Those of mechanics—each one singing his, as it should be, blithe and strong;
The carpenter singing his, as he measures his plank or beam,
The mason singing his, as he makes ready for work, or leaves off work;
The boatman singing what belongs to him in his boat—the deckhand singing on the steamboat deck;
The shoemaker singing as he sits on his bench—the hatter singing as he stands;
The wood-cutter's song—the ploughboy's, on his way in the morning,
Or at the noon intermission, or at sundown;
The delicious singing of the mother—or of the young wife at work—or of the girl sewing and
   washing—each singing what belongs to her, and to none else;
The day what belongs to the day—At night, the party of young fellows, robust, friendly,
Singing, with open mouths, their strong melodious songs.

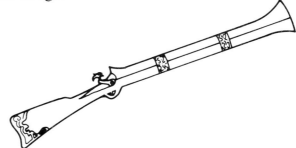

Concord Hymn
Ralph Waldo Emerson

By the rude bridge that arched the flood,
   Their flag to April's breeze unfurled,
Here once the embattled farmers stood,
   And fired a shot heard around the world.

The foe long since the silence slept;
   Alike the conqueror silent sleeps;
And time the ruined bridge has slept
   Down the dark stream which seaward creeps.

On this green bank, by this soft stream,
   We set to-day a votive stone;
That memory may their deed redeem,
   When, like our sires, our sons are gone.

Spirit, that made those heroes dare
   To die, or leave their children free,
Bid Time and Nature gently spare
   The shaft we raise to them and thee.

The Bee
Isaac Watts

How doth the little busy Bee
   Improve each shining Hour,
And gather Honey all day
   From every opening Flower!

How skillfully she builds her Cell!
   How neat she spreads the Wax!
And labours hard to store it well
   With the sweet Food she makes.

In Works of Labour or of Skill
   I would be busy too:
For Satan finds some Mischief still
   For idle Hands to do.

In Books, or Work, or healthful Play
   Let my first Years be past,
That I may give for every Day
   Some good Account at last.

Song of Life
Charles MacKay

A traveler on a dusty road
  Strewed acorns on the lea;
And one took root and sprouted up,
  And grew into a tree.
Love sought its shade at evening time,
  To breathe its early vows;
And Age was pleased, in heights of noon,
  To bask beneath its boughs.
The dormouse loved its dangling twigs,
  The birds sweet music bore—
It stood a glory in its place,

A little spring had lost its way
  Amid the grass and fern;
A passing stranger scooped a well
  Where weary men might turn.
He walled it in, and hung with care
  A ladle on the brink;
He thought not of the deed he did,
  But judged that Toil might drink.
He passed again; and lo! the well,
  By summer never dried,
Had cooled ten thousand parched tongues,
  And saved a life beside.

A nameless man, amid the crowd
  That thronged the daily mart,
Let fall a word of hope and love,
  Unstudied from the heart,
A whisper of the tumult thrown,
  A transitory breath,
It raised a brother from the dust,
  It saved a sould from death.
O herm! O fount! O word of love!
  O thought at random cast!
Ye were but little at the first,
  But mighty at the last.

Citizenship
Anonymous

A flag waves o'er me.
The power of its image
Stirs my pride and heart.

Strength in Union
Alice Crowell Hoffman

Many, many tiny threads,
  Each weak if used alone,
Woven tightly have become
  The finest banner known.
Many, many people, too,
  Of ev'ry walk and station,
Bound in love with purpose true,
  Make us a mighty nation.

Written in the Album of a Child
William Wordsworth

Small service is true service while it lasts;
Of friends, however humble, scorn not one:
The daisy, by the shadow that it casts,
Protects the lingering dew-drop from the sun.

Perseverance

Believing in Yourself
Anonymous

There may be days
when you get up in the morning
and things aren't the way
you had hoped they would be.
That's when you have to tell yourself that
   things will get better.
There are times when people
disappoint you and let you down,
but those are the times
when you must remind yourself
to keep your life focused on believing in
   yourself
and all that you are capable of.
There will be challenges to face
and changes to make in your life,
and it is up to you to accept them.
Constantly keep yourself headed
in the right direction for you.
It may not be easy at times,
but in those times of struggle
you will find a stronger sense of who you are.
So when the days come that are filled
with frustration and unexpected
   responsibilities,
remember to believe in yourself
and all you want your life to be,
because the challenges and changes
will only help you to find the goals
that you know are meant to come true for you.

Perseverance
is making a
continuing,
effort.

A Tragic Story
William Makepeace Thackery

There lived a sage in days of yore,
   And he a handsome pigtail wore;
But wondered much and sorrowed more,
   Because it hung behind him.

He mused upon this curious case,
   And swore he'd changed the pigtail's place,
And have it hanging at his face,
   Not dangling there behind him.

Then round and round, and out and in,
   All day— the puzzled sage did spin;
In vain it mattered not a pin—
   The pigtail hung behind him.

And right and left and round about,
   And up and down and in and out
He turned; but still the pigtail stout
   Hung steadily behind him.

And though his efforts never slack,
   And though he twist and twirl, and tack
Alas! Still faithful to his back,
   The pigtail hangs behind him.

The Village Blacksmith

Henry Wadsworth Longfellow

Under a spreading chestnut tree
   The village smithy stands;
The smith, a mighty man is he,
   With large and sinewy hands;
And muscles of his brawny arms
   Are strong as iron bands.

His hair is crisp, and black, and long,
   His face is like the tan;
His brow is wet with honest sweat,
   He earns whatever he can,
And looks the whole world in the face,
   For he owes not any man.

Week in, week out, from morn till night,
   You can hear the bellows blow;
You can hear him swing his heavy sledge,
   With measured beat and slow,
Like a sexton ringing the village bell,
   When the evening sun is low.
And children coming home from school
   Look in the open door;
They love to see the flaming forge,
   And hear the bellows roar,
And catch the burning sparks that fly
   Like chaff from a threshing floor.

He goes on Sunday to church,
   And sits among the boys;
He hears the parson prayer and preach,
   He hears his daughter's voice,
Singing in the village choir,
   And it makes his heart rejoice.

It sounds to him like her mother's voice,
   Singing in Paradise.
He needs must think of her once more,
   How in the grave she lies;
And with his hard, rough hand he wipes
   A tear out of his eyes.

Toiling, rejoicing, sorrowing,
   Onward through life he goes;
Each morning sees some task begun,
   Each evening sees it close;
Something attempted, something done,
   Has earned a night's repose.

Persevere
McGuffy's Reader

The fisher who draws in his net too soon,
  Won't have any fish to sell;
The child who shuts up his book too soon,
  Won't learn any lesson well.

If you would have your learning stay,
  Be patient—don't learn too fast;
The man who travels a mile each day,
  May get round the world at last.

I Think I Can
Anonymous

If you think you are beaten you are;
If you think you dare not, you don't;
If you want to win but think you can't;
It's almost a cinch you won't.

If you think you'll lose you're lost;
For out of the world we find
Success begins with a fellow's will
It's all in a state of mind.

Life's battles don't always go
To the stronger and faster man,
But sooner or later the man who wins
Is the man who thinks he can.

Meanings
Anonymous

Standing for what you believe in,
Regardless of the odds against you,
and the pressure that tears at your resistance,
          …means courage.

Keeping a smile on your face,
When inside you feel like dying,
For the sake of supporting others,
          …means strength.

Doing more than is expected,
To make another's life a little more bearable,
Without uttering a single complaint,
          …means compassion.

Helping a friend in need,
No matter the time or the effort,
To the best of your ability,
          …means loyalty.

Giving more than you have,
And expecting nothing,
But nothing in return,
          …means selflessness.

Holding your head high,
And being the best you know you can be
When life seems to fall apart at your feet,
Facing each difficulty with the confidence
That time will bring you better tomorrows,
And never giving up,
          …means confidence.

Perseverance
Anonymous

  A bird from its nest
First flight in a wintry sky.
  Soar soon with eagles.

Stopping By Woods on a Snowy Evening
Robert Frost

Whose woods these are I think I know.
    His house is in the village though;
He will not see me stopping here
    To watch his woods fill up with snow.

My little horse must think it queer
    To stop without a farmhouse near
Between the woods and frozen lake
    The darkest evening of the year.

He gives his harness bells a shake
    To ask if there is some mistake.
The only other sound's the sweep
    Of easy wind and downy flake.

The woods are lovely, dark and deep.
    But I have promises to keep,
And miles to go before I sleep,
    And miles to go before I sleep.

Perseverance
Johann Wolfgang von Goethe

We must not hope to be mowers,
    And to gather the ripe gold ears,
Unless we have first been sowers
    And watered the furrows with tears.

It is not just as we take it,
    This mystical world of ours,
Life's field will yield as we make it
    A harvest of thorns or of flowers.

Try, Try Again
T. H. Palmer

'Tis a lesson you should heed,
Try, try again;
If at first you don't succeed,
Try, try again;
Then your courage should appear,
For if you will persevere,
You will conquer, never fear;
Try, try again.

The Winds of Fate
Ella Wheeler Wilcox

One ship drives east and another drives west
    With the selfsame winds that blow.
Tis the set of sails
    And not the gales
Which tell us the way to go.

Like winds of the seas are the ways of fate,
    As we voyage along through the life:
That decides its goal,
    And not the calm or the strife.

Carry On!
Robert Service

It's easy to fight when everything's right,
And you're mad with the thrill and the glory;
It's easy to cheer when victory's near,
And wallow in fields that are gory.
It's a different song when everything's wrong,
When you're feeling infernally mortal;
When it's ten against one, and hope there
   is none,
Buck up, little soldier, and chortle:

Carry on! Carry on!
There isn't much punch in your blow.
You're glaring and staring and hitting out blind;
You're muddy and bloody, but never you mind.
Carry on! Carry on!
You haven't the ghost of a show.
It's looking like death, but while you've a
   breath,
Carry on, my son! Carry on!

And so in the strife of the battle of life
It's easy to fight when you're winning;
It's easy to slave, and starve and be brave,
When the dawn of success is beginning.
But the man who can meet despair and defeat
With cheer, there's the man of God's choosing;
The man who can fight to Heaven's own height
Is the man who can fight when he's losing.

Carry on! Carry on!
Things never were looming so black.
But show that you haven't a cowardly streak,
And though you're unlucky you never are weak.
Carry on! Carry on!
Brace up for another attack.
It's looking like hell, but—you never can tell:
Carry on, old man! Carry on!

There are some who drift in the deserts of doubt,
And some who in brutishness wallow;
There are others, I know, who in piety go
Because of a Heaven to follow.
But to labor with zest, and to give of your best,
For the sweetness and joy of the giving;
To help folks along with hand and a song;
Why, there's the real sunshine of living.

Carry on! Carry on!
Fight the good fight and true;
Believe in your mission, greet life with a cheer;
There's big work to do, and that's why you
   are here.
Carry on! Carry on!
Let the world be the better for you;
And at last when you die, let this be your cry:
Carry on, my soul! Carry on!

I Stepped from Plank to Plank
Emily Dickinson

I stepped from plank to plank
So slow and cautiously;
The stars about my head I felt,
About my feet the sea.

I knew not but the next
Would be my final inch,—
This gave me that precarious gait
Some call experience.

Our Lips and Ears
Anonymous

If you your lips would keep from slips,
Five things observe with care:
Of whom you speak, to whom you speak,
And how and when and where.

I you your ears would save from jeers,
These things keep meekly hid:
Myself and I, and mine and my,
And how I do and did.

"Hope" is the Things with Feathers
Emily Dickinson

"Hope" is the thing with feathers—
And sings the tune without the words—
And never stops—at all—
And sweetest—in the Gale—is heard—
And sore must be the storm—
That could abash the little Bird
That kept so many warm—
I've heard in the chillest land—
And on the strangest Sea—
Yet, never, in Extremity,
It asked a crumb—Of Me.

Upon a Snail
John Bunyan

She goes but softly, but she goeth sure,
She stumbles not, as stronger creatures do;
Her journey's shorter, so she may endure
Better than they which do much further go.

She makes no noise, but stilly seizeth on
The flower or herb appointed for her food;
The which she quietly doth feed upon,
While others range, and glare, but find no good.

And though she doth but very softly go,
However slow her pace be, yet 'tis sure;
And certainly they that do travel so,
The prize which they do aim at, they procure.

Responsibility

A responsible person takes care of himself and fulfills his obligations.

The Sin of Omission
Margaret E. Sangster

It isn't the thing you do, dear,
  It's the thing you leave undone
That gives you a bit of heartache
  At setting of the sun.
The tender word forgotten,
  The letter you did not write,
The flowers you did not send, dear,
  Are your haunting ghosts at night.

The stone you might have lifted
  Out of a brother's way;
The bit of heartsome counsel
  You were hurried too much to say;
The loving touch of the hand, dear,
  The gentle, winning tone
Which you had no time or thought for
  With troubles enough of your own.

Those little acts of kindness
  So easily out of mind,
Those chances to be angels
  Which poor mortals find—
They come in night and silence,
  Each sad, reproachful wraith,
When hope is faint and flagging,
  And a chill has fallen on faith.

For life is all too short, dear,
  And sorrow is all too great,
To suffer our slow compassion
  That tarries until too late;
And it isn't the thing you do, dear,
  It's the thing you leave undone
Which gives you a bit of a heartache
  At the setting of the sun.

Mr. Nobody
Anonymous

I know a funny little man,
  As quiet as a mouse,
Who does the mischief that is done
  In everybody's house!
There's no one ever sees his face,
  And yet we all agree
That every plate we break was cracked
  By Mr. Nobody.

'Tis he who always tears our books,
  Who leaves the door ajar,
He pulls the buttons from our shirts,
  And scatters pins afar;
That squeaking door will always squeak,
  For, prithee, don't you see,
We leave the oiling to be done
  By Mr. Nobody.

The finger marks upon the door
  By none of us are made;
We never leave the blinds unclosed,
  To let the curtains fade.
The ink we never spill; the boots
  That lying round you see
Are not our boots—they all belong
  To Mr. Nobody.

Which Loved Best?
Joy Allison

"I love you Mother," said little John;
Then, forgetting his work, his cap went on,
And he was off to the garden swing,
And left her the water and wood to bring.
"I love you, Mother," said rosy Nell—
"I love you better than tongue can tell";
Then she teased and pouted full half the day,
Till her mother rejoiced when she went to
   play.
"I love you Mother," said little Fan;
"Today I'll help you all I can;
How glad I am that school doesn't keep!"
So she rocked the babe till it fell asleep.

Then, stepping softly, she fetched the
   broom,
And swept the floor and tidied the room;
Busy and happy all day was she,
Helpful and happy as child could be.
"I love you, Mother," again they said,
Three little children going to bed;
How do you think that mother guessed
Which one really loved her best?

Loss and Gain
Henry Wadsworth Longfellow

When I compare
   What I have lost with what I have gained,
What I have missed with what attained,
   Little room do I find for pride
I am aware
   How many days have been idly spent;
How like an arrow the good intent
   Has fallen short or been turned aside.
But who shall dare
   To measure loss and gain in this wise?
Defeat may be victory in disquiet;
   The lowest ebb is the turn of the tide.

Count That Day Lost
George Eliot

If you sit down at set of sun
   And count the acts that you have done,
And, counting, find
   One self-denying deed, one word
That eased the heart of him who heard,
   One glance most kind
That fell like sunshine where it went—
   Then you may count that day well spent.

But if, through all the livelong day,
   You've cheered no heart, by yea or nay—
If, through it all
   You've nothing done that you can trace
That brought the sunshine to one face—
   No act most small
That helped some soul and nothing cost—
   Then count that day as worse than lost.

An Oyster
Anonymous

There once was an oyster
Whose story I tell,
Who found that some sand
Had got into his shell.

It was only a grain,
But it gave him great pain.
For oysters have feelings
Although they're so plain.

Now, did he berate
The harsh workings of fate
That had brought him
To such a deplorable state?

Did her curse at the government,
Cry for election,
And claim that the sea should
Have given him protection?

"No," he said to himself
As he lay on a shell,
Since I cannot remove it,
I shall try to improve it.

Now the years have rolled around,
As the years always do,
And he came to his ultimate
Destiny—stew.

And the small grain of sand
That had bothered him so
Was a beautiful pearl
All richly aglow.

Now the tale has a moral,
For isn't it grand
What an oyster can do
With a morsel of sand?

What couldn't we do
If we'd only begin
With some of the things
That get under our skin.

How to Be Happy
Anonymous

Are you almost disgusted with life, little
  man?
I'll tell you a wonderful trick
That will bring you contentment, if
  anything can
Do something for somebody, quick!

Are you awfully tired with play, little girl?
Wearied, discouraged, and sick—
I'll tell you the loveliest game in the world,
Do something for somebody quick!

Though it rains like the rain of the floods,
  little man
And the clouds are forbidding and thick,
You can make the sun shine in your soul,
  little man
Do something for somebody, quick!

Though the stars are like brass overhead,
  little girl,
And the walks like a well-heated brick
And our earthly affairs in a terrible whirl,
Do something for somebody, quick!

Little Boy Blue
Mother Goose

Little Boy Blue, come blow your horn,
The sheep's in the meadow, the cow's in the
  corn.
Where is the boy who looks after the
  sheep?
He's under a haycock, fast asleep.
Will you wake him? No, not I,
For if I do, he's sure to cry.

It's Up to You
Anonymous

One song can spark a moment,
One flower can wake the dream.

One tree can start a forest,
One bird can herald spring.

One smile begins a friendship,
One handclasp lifts a soul.

One star can guide a ship at sea,
One word can frame the goal.

One vote can change a nation,
One sunbeam lights a room.

One candle wipes out darkness,
One laugh will conquer gloom.

One step must start each journey,
One word must start each prayer.

One hope will raise our spirits,
One touch can show you care.

One voice can speak with wisdom,
One heart can know what's true.

One life can make the difference,
You see, IT'S UP TO YOU.

For Want of a Nail
Anonymous

For want of a nail, a shoe was lost,
For want of a shoe, a horse was lost
For want of a horse, a battle was lost,
For want of a battle, a kingdom was lost,
And all for the want of a horseshoe nail.

The Hump
Rudyard Kipling

The Camel's hump is an ugly lump
Which well you may see at the Zoo;
But uglier yet is the hump we get
From having too little to do.

Kiddies and grown-ups too-oo-oo,
If we haven't enough to do-oo-oo,
We get the hump—
Cameelious hump—
The hump that is black and blue.

We climb out of bed with a frouzly head,
And a snarly-yarly voice.
We shiver and scowl and we grunt and we growl
At our bath and our boots and our toys;

And there ought to be a corner for me
(And I know there is one for you)
When we get the hump—Cameelious hump—
The hump that is black and blue!

The cure for this ill is not to sit still,
Or frowst with a book by the fire;
But to take a large hoe and a shovel also,
And dig till you gently perspire;

And then you will find that the sun and the wind,
And the Djinn of the Garden too,
Have lifted the hump—
The horrible hump—
The hump that is black and blue!

I get it as well as you-oo-oo
If I haven't enough to do-oo-oo!
We all get hump—
Cameelious hump—
Kiddies and grown-ups too!

Index of Poems

Index of Poets & Sources